Affirmations

to Change and Heal Your Life

Also by Vicky Thurlow

Books
Dowsing for Answers and Healing
Changing the Face of God

Audio/CD
Guided Meditations:
Experience Joy
Achieve Your Goals
Increase Confidence
Increase Love, Faith, and Trust
Increase Creativity and Self-Expression
Break Bad Habits and Addictions
Inner Peace, Security, and Spiritual Awakenings
Rest for the Mind, Body, and Sprit
Morning Meditation/Peaceful Sleep
Healing Meditation
Guided Meditation Series

Visual/DVD
BreaThin—Effective Breathing Techniques

For more information about Vicky Thurlow's work, books,
guided meditations, CDs, DVDs, workshops, and healing resources,
please visit her Web site, http://www.pursuitofhealing.com.

Affirmations
to Change and Heal Your Life
Emotionally, Physically, and Spiritually

Vicky Thurlow

DVT

Grand Junction, Colorado

This book is not intended as medical advice and the author does not dispense medical or psychological advice or prescribe the use of any technique as a form of treatment without the advice of a physician. The author's intent is to offer information in general to help in emotional, physical, and spiritual growth. The author assumes no responsibility for your actions should you choose to use any techniques or suggestions.

Published by
DVT Investments
2800 Printers Way
Grand Junction, Colorado 81506

Publisher's Cataloging-in-Publication Data
Thurlow, Vicky.

Affirmations to change and heal your life : emotionally, physically, and spiritually / Vicky Thurlow.—Grand Junction, Colo. : DVT Investments, 2008.

p. ; cm.

ISBN: 978-0-9816480-5-7

1. Self-actualization (Psychology) 2. Change (Psychology) 3. Mind and body. 4. Well-being — Psychological aspects. I. Title.

BF637.S4 T483 2008
158—dc22   2008928948

Project coordination by Jenkins Group, Inc
www.BookPublishing.com
Interior design by Brooke Camfield

Printed in the United States of America
by Colorado Printing Company, Grand Junction, Colorado

12 11 10 09 08 • 5 4 3 2 1

CONTENTS

EXERCISES

INTRODUCTION

G ranted, there will always be situations in life where you have no control, but the manner in which **you** deal with those situations is **your choice** and **your responsibility,** no one else's. It's important for you to realize that **you** are in charge of **your choices. You** are also in charge of how **you choose** to react to any situation you encounter. If you choose to blame someone else for things not going right in your life, **you** are making the choice to be a victim. Likewise, if **you** choose to give credit to someone for something you have accomplished, **you** are choosing to discredit yourself which I call false humility. These are only two examples are very subtle yet deep and critically important core beliefs and emotions that limit and disempower people every day.

Many people go through life unaware that they have limiting beliefs and therefore continue to live their life disempowered instead of empowered.

This book gives you tools that will help you identify your core beliefs; whether they are empowering or disempowering. It will teach you how to change the beliefs that you then know need to be changed, so that you can begin to live the best life imaginable.

By becoming aware of your beliefs and learning how to change them from disempowering to empowering through positive words or affirmations, you can gain the ability to completely change and heal your life emotionally, physically, and spiritually. I truly hope that this will be the beginning or the continuation of your pursuit of healing.

Here's the simple and straight forward truth: if you're unhappy, miserable, poor, overweight, or unhealthy, it's because of the beliefs you live with, the choices you are making and the words you are speaking. If you're happy, healthy, and enjoying financial success, it's because of the healthy beliefs you have, the choices you are making and the words you are speaking. The quality of your life is **your** choice and **you** alone have the Power to have whatever **you** desire. I'm here to help you figure out how to get it.

I venture to say that there isn't anyone in your life who stands over you and forces you to overeat. Am I right? If you overeat on a regular basis it's because **you** choose to overeat. The great news is **you** can choose to stop. Likewise if you don't exercise on a regular basis it's because **you** are choosing not to. The great news again is **you** can choose to get yourself out of bed each morning and burn some calories (sounds better then working out doesn't it?). If you don't have a job you enjoy or you're not making the amount of money you desire, stop blaming other people and figure out what **you** can do to get your dream job that pays you what you think you deserve.

I encourage you to take the time and do all of the exercises in this book. It's your responsibility to find out what beliefs you may be operating under that are keeping you from achieving all you are capable of. Then be determined to follow through with a plan for change. When you take responsibility for everything in your life including your beliefs, thoughts, and the words you speak every day, you can live an empowered, fulfilled and exciting life. No one else can do any of this for you. It's all up to **you**, and it's all **your** choice.

You may be wondering "What does this all mean? How do I take responsibility for everything in my life? How do I change my life long beliefs and control my thoughts?" You first begin by addressing your belief system and find out exactly what it is you believe about as many different subjects as you can. Then you will need to become aware of your thoughts and also the words you speak throughout each and every day. Once you understand that the words you speak are the exact representation of your beliefs, emotions, and your thoughts and that they create your reality, you'll no doubt realize that you want to make some changes and *fast*.

Remember, no one has control over your words, thoughts or beliefs so that means only **you** are one hundred percent in charge of your reality. If you are living in a reality that you enjoy, it's because **your** thoughts, beliefs, and words have created it and **you** need to take credit for that. If you are living in a nightmare reality, it's because **your** thoughts, beliefs, and words have created it and **you** can change it. Your words are full of life changing Power and if you need change in your life emotionally, financially, socially, physically, or spiritually, you've picked up the right book.

*Whatever **you** choose to speak, you will get, and what you get is ultimately **your** choice because **you are in charge!***

CHAPTER 1

THE POWER OF YOUR
BELIEFS AND THOUGHTS

*Whatever you believe and
think you are, that you are.*
~Vicky~

Whatever you believe, think, and speak about your reality; is exactly what your reality is. For instance, if you believe, think, and speak words that say you have a pretty good life, you have a pretty good life. If you believe, think, and speak words that say you have a great life, you experience a great life. If you believe, think, and say that your life is a mess, meaningless, and nothing goes right, then your life is a mess, meaningless, and nothing goes right for you.

What if I told you that you have the Power to change your reality? You have the Power to change your reality! If you want to change it for the better, you will begin by changing what you believe, what you think, and what you speak (your affirmations).

You begin by first becoming aware of your belief system which creates your thoughts and emotions. Those thoughts and emotions slip out of your mouth pretty easily without much awareness. This all creates your reality. This concept is not difficult to understand; so why don't more people take control and make changes in their lives? Because it takes effort and discipline to do self-work. If you truly want to change your reality, you must learn to change your beliefs, thoughts, and words.

I have found it to be quite common, while coaching individuals over the years, for them to suddenly realize they don't even know what they believe about certain things. They suddenly become aware that they have been living their lives based on beliefs that were their parent's, a person in authority over them, or even sometimes their churches. It's extremely important for you to know exactly what **you** believe about money, relationships, work, success, failure, God, religion, and yourself because if you're not getting what you want out of life, it's because your current beliefs are not empowering you or assisting you. Once you become aware of what those beliefs are, you can change them to ones that will empower your efforts. That's when you can begin to get and experience what you want in any area of your life. It isn't complicated. It just takes a little time and effort.

Once you begin to do the work involved in changing your old beliefs into new ones, you will begin to notice your thoughts and emotions shifting as well. Even your words will begin to reflect your new way of thinking. That's when your life really begins to rock!

There may be times during your transformation, when you will need to speak words first to convince yourself (your conscious and subconscious mind) of a new belief instead of the other way around. But regardless of which comes first, beliefs or words, they are **your** affirmations and they will create **your** life or **your** reality. You and I and everyone we know speak affirmations all day long whether we are aware of them or not. Unfortunately, not many people take the time to become aware of what's coming out of their mouth as an affirmation let alone take the time to really know what they believe. It takes determination and practice to become aware of what needs to be changed in your life and it takes even more work to speak words that reflect those beliefs . . . but it is not impossible. With a little practice it becomes easier and easier, and as it does, your life gets better and better.

Let's begin by asking a few questions. Do you know what your beliefs are concerning money? What do you believe about marriage, sex, work, God, or even the Bible? Have you ever written out your beliefs? You may be surprised by what you actually believe about certain subjects when you take the time to ask yourself and then write it down. We'll do this in a little bit. Many people who do this work are surprised to find that they had no idea they believe what they believe. Others realize they have been operating under their parent's beliefs but when it came right down to it, they didn't personally believe what their parents believed; they have just been on auto pilot since childhood. They are people who have never taken the time to form their own beliefs. They are people who are not living their best life.

Your beliefs are your perceptions about a given subject and those beliefs are charged with memories and emotions. Everyone gets his beliefs from somewhere and I believe there are three reasons why you believe what you believe.

Reason number one I call **Childhood Conditioning**. As a young child, you simply took in everything you were told either by parents, adults, or a church, good or bad. Now as an adult, you have never taken the time to question any of those beliefs. You may (or may not) have been programmed with fear and guilt growing up. You may have been told that you were worthless or stupid and would never amount to anything. Maybe you have old beliefs about money that are keeping you from following your passion. Regardless of where they came from or what your old beliefs are, you simply haven't taken the time to be *aware* of what you were taught or what you were indoctrinated with, whether it was good for you or not. You are on auto pilot.

The second reason is what I call **Controlled Conditioning**. This is when an adult agrees to live and operate by someone else's beliefs based on their personal safety, lack of self-confidence, or fear of salvation. This could be an abusive intimate relationship, kidnapping, or abusive religious brainwashing. This is when you allow yourself to be deceived by fabricated promises with an underlying tone of fear. You are led to believe that you cannot exist without them and if you tried, you would most certainly die.

The third reason is the healthiest and most empowering reason: you believe what you believe because you are **self-realized**. Self-realization is the *realization* that you have choices. It's when you *realize* that you do not have to live your life in fear of losing your salvation, in fear of God, or in fear of an abuser. It's when you *realize* that you can make your own decisions, have your own beliefs, and that you won't die. You *realize* that you have personal power and you use it. You *realize* you have freedom. This personal power comes only through taking time for inner-reflection. This isn't to say that you can't have some of the same beliefs as other people do, but the difference between self-*realized* beliefs and controlled or conditioned beliefs is you are making a conscious decision to believe empowering beliefs based on what's best for you without judgment, fear, or guilt.

Unhappiness and an unfulfilled life are products of a disempowering belief system. Happiness and a life of contentment are products of an empowering belief system. They are both a choice. Which do you want?

I'm going to share a few exercises to help you become aware of your beliefs, what thoughts are mulling around in your head, and what words you are speaking that are ultimately creating your reality. After you've completed the exercises and if you decide you like your life or your reality the way it is, your work will be finished. If, on the other hand, you decide you want a better life and you realize that your current beliefs aren't supporting you, continue the exercises in this book, and we will begin to change what needs to be changed in order for you to live the life you want.

Exercise 1.1

Be aware of your words throughout the day and write them down.

First I want you to become aware of what you're saying throughout each day. Observe what comes out of your mouth when you are talking about your health, job, or your children. It will be helpful if you write your phrases down in a notebook so later on you will see just how much changing you have done by the time you finish this short book.

As you give attention to and write down your words, you will begin to understand why your reality is what it is. Your reality and your belief system all come out your mouth in the form of words or affirmations. This is the best place for you to begin if you want to create a different life, improve your heath, earn more money, or have better relationships.

For example, when you say something like, "I'll never have a body like hers," that is an affirmation of what you are thinking. You may or may not actually believe that though. If you keep using those words, you can be sure that you will *never* have a body like hers. On the other hand, if you change your words, thoughts, and actions, your beliefs will follow suit. Your new thoughts will be that if you work as hard as she does, you will have a body as good as hers. Your affirmation or words could be something like: "I'm going to do everything in my power to have a body like hers." Now those words reflect a belief that says it's at least possible and that you are willing to work for it.

Another example of an affirmation or belief is, "I never seem to make enough money to get out of debt," or "I'll never get this house paid off, something is always breaking." Well, as long as you think that and as long as you continue to affirm those thoughts and beliefs by speaking those words, you're exactly right, you won't ever make enough money, you'll never get out of debt, and something will always be breaking around your house. Your subconscious mind will find ways to always keep you in debt and keep you from making the money you deserve to make. Have you ever heard yourself or other people say, "I hate my job," "I'm so fat," "I never can get a lucky break," or "I just can't get ahead?" If you've ever said those things you need to stop immediately! Make a pact with yourself to NEVER say those words again even if you do believe them. It may take a little time to change your thoughts and old beliefs, but they can be changed. You begin changing them by changing your words. Your words are extremely powerful!

The reason words and thoughts are so incredibly powerful is that they vibrate with Energy. The Energy they vibrate with attracts 'like' Energy and brings about exactly what your words are saying and what your thoughts are thinking. In other words, what you say, you get; what you send out in thought, you get back. This is known as the Universal Law of Attraction, and it works one hundred percent of the time and is no respecter of persons. If you speak words of fear, such as, "I'm scared to death of spiders," you will continue to have fear of spiders and will end up drawing more spiders into your world. If you continue your affirmation that you're scared to death, you will attract more situations in your life that will scare you to death. If you speak words of lack, you will have lack in your life. If you speak words of success, such as, "I am successful at whatever I put my mind to," you will draw situations to you that will cause you to be successful. If you speak works of prosperity, you will have a prosperous life. It's really not very difficult to get what you want once you understand the Law of Attraction and are willing to do a little work.

You now can understand the two choices you have. Choice number one is continuing to live with disempowering beliefs and thoughts and speaking words that affirm those beliefs and thoughts. Choice number two is taking the necessary steps to change your disempowering beliefs and thoughts into empowering ones, then to speak those new beliefs and thoughts daily to attract positive situations into your life. It's that simple. You must be willing to change what you speak and what you think!

I believe that everyone has at least one disempowering belief that keeps them from doing, being, or having what they want. If the truth be known, most people have more than one. I also believe that everyone is responsible for his own beliefs. If you want to know who your authentic self is and want to live a better life, you must do the work it takes to change your beliefs from disempowering to empowering.

You do realize that there is no one who can do this work for you; it's up to you. So, beginning right now, pay attention to the words you speak. Make a conscious decision to be aware of what comes out of your mouth over the next several days and write it all down.

When I began listening to my words and I started asking myself questions about what my beliefs were concerning different areas of my life, money was one of the subjects that immediately came up. When I asked myself what I really believed about money, I instantly went back in time to when I was growing up. I heard things like:

Money doesn't grow on trees.
Money isn't everything.
We'll never be able to afford that.
If God wanted you to be rich, you would have been born with money.
You have to work your fingers to the bone just to make ends meet.
Put some money away for a rainy day; you never know what might happen.
It's better to give than to receive.
Rich people are snobs.
Jesus was poor.
And my all time favorite: Money is the root of all evil.

Now where did all that come from? The Bible says in 1 Timothy 6:10, that, "The *love* of money is the root of all evil." It does not say that *money* is the root. It says the *love* of money. Since we're on the subject, if you simply go through and take things out of context, as all religions do, in order to support their doctrines, you can make the Bible say anything you want it to say. In Ecclesiastes 10:10, it says, "Money is the answer to everything." Look it up. Since so many people strive to be just like Jesus, it only makes sense that people harbor the belief that being poor is more "God like" than being rich. But just a second! Nowhere in the Bible does it say that Jesus was poor. In fact, it says the opposite. Of course, the Bible is so full of inconsistencies and contradictions that it's hard to find definitive answers about anything. But it does say that Joseph, the father of Jesus, came from a wealthy family. Why do you think he and Mary were on their way to Bethlehem? They had to go pay taxes. Pay taxes on what? You don't pay taxes if you don't own anything. Even if Joseph didn't have money, Jesus was given very expensive gifts by the magi (astrologers) when he was born. They gave him "treasures, gifts of gold, frankincense, and myrrh." Matthew 2:11. That was enough wealth to last a lifetime. Jesus was not poor. To think I believed that for so many years.

What did you hear about money? Do you believe what you were told, or do you actually have different beliefs, but haven't acknowledged them or consciously changed them? This is what I'm asking you to do now: question your old beliefs and change them if they don't empower your life.

It's now time to ask yourself some tough questions, and it's time for you to find out what you really think about things. What are your core beliefs? Do you operate by what you were always told? What if what you have been told isn't true for you any longer? Here's a biggy: What are you afraid of? What do you fear will happen if you change your mind about the way you've always believed about something? It's important that you know the answer to that question.

Being judged and being judged unfairly (injustice) was a very big fear in my life up and into my forties. Whether my fear came from religious teachings in this lifetime, or possibly cellular memory from another lifetime, I don't really know. What I do know is that my fear was being caused by my beliefs. I had to find out what those beliefs were and then change them in order to face my fears. When I changed my beliefs, the fear just went away.

I also grew up with a tremendous amount of fear about dying. I had been taught by the Seventh Day Adventist church that if you were "good enough" in God's opinion, you would go to heaven. If you were not, you would go to hell. But what was even scarier was that you wouldn't know until long after you died. When Jesus returns at the "Second Coming," you would then be *judged* in front of everyone, as if in a trial. Well, living in a no-win situation, as you do in the Seventh Day Adventist church and most religions, I always knew I was going to fail the test or judgment of God and go straight to hell. This was a core belief under which I was living my life and it was disempowering to me in more ways than one. I wasn't *aware* of this belief nor was I *aware* of how it was affecting me until I began to question these beliefs I had about judgment during a lawsuit I went through. When I questioned this particular belief, I *realized* I didn't really believe it. I just operated under it. I couldn't change it because I wasn't *aware* of it or that it even needed changing. The lawsuit I found myself in woke me up and made me *realize* what needed to be changed. When I became *aware* of the disempowering beliefs that I had, I was then able to take the time to consciously change them. By changing what I believed, I freed myself from disempowering and fearful thoughts, and I empowered myself by living by my own beliefs.

Even though I've changed my beliefs about judgment, I still don't enjoy being judged. Of course no one does. Now when someone judges me, it doesn't disempower me like it used to. What I've learned and what I hope I can clearly get across to you is that you must find out what you are afraid of. Ask yourself why you're afraid. Examine the beliefs.

Ask why you believe what you believe. Finally, change your beliefs if you need to so they will empower you instead of disempower you.

As I've mentioned before, the journey of self-discovery or inner-discovery is the best place to begin by asking yourself what beliefs you currently have or what you have been taught concerning particular subjects and then writing them down.

As you do this work I want you to question the validity of each belief you have written down. When I asked myself questions and then wrote what I believed about death, I wondered how I could ever have believed such nonsense. I had just never really taken the time to think about such concepts. I certainly no longer wanted to believe that I and everything about me would cease to exist when I die. Over the years I had heard and read story after story about people from all different parts of the world, who all had similar near-death experiences. According to each of the stories I read, there was something that existed, something that was experienced after death or these people would not all have similar stories. I began to scrutinize what I had been taught. Then I made up my own mind. I chose to change my old belief about death.

Here are some helpful steps in gaining *awareness* of what some of your beliefs are. Again, it might be helpful to do the following exercises in a notebook so that you can refer to it for years to come.

Exercise 1.2

Write some of your core beliefs you've been taught in column one.

Take a few moments right now to write out some of your core beliefs. In a notebook, begin by making two columns. In the first column write down what first comes to your mind concerning different subjects. Write what you've been taught since childhood. Write the first thing that little voice in your head says to you and don't stop with one or two things. Column one will probably be the beliefs that you operate under. Here are some subjects and examples to get you started. If you have a dozen thoughts on each subject, by all means, write them all down.

What do I believe or what have I been taught about money?

Example: Money is the root of all evil. Money doesn't grow on trees. Only the rich get richer. Maybe you believe that money is good.

Write your own thoughts:

What do I believe or what have I been taught about sex?

Example: Sex just gets people into trouble. Sex is just for men to enjoy. Sex is wrong before marriage.

Write your own thoughts:

What do I believe or what have I been taught about work?

Example: You have to work your fingers to the bone or you're nothing. You'll have to work until the day you die. No matter how hard I work, I'll never get ahead.

Write your own thoughts:

What do I believe or what have I been taught about security?

Example: I will always have enough. Women can never make as much as men.

Write your own thoughts:

Exercise 1.3

Write your true beliefs in column two.

Now that you have written what the voices in your head immediately said and what beliefs you probably live your life by concerning each of these subjects, I'd like you to take a moment to think about each subject again only from a different point of view. First of all I want you to close your eyes, sit back in your chair and take a couple of deep breaths in through your nose and out through your mouth. Open your eyes and continue. Did you do it? If not, do it now. Take a deep breath.

Okay, now just like before, I want you to ask yourself the same questions. This time, write your answers down in column two. Remember, column one is what the little voice in your head chattered at you immediately. Column two is what you think when you turn that voice off and listen to your own.

For example: If you wrote down, money is evil in column one, ask yourself again. Is it really? Do I really believe that money is evil or was that my parent's belief or my church's belief? Then, in column two, write what **you** believe without listening to that little voice in your head. Hit the mute button for a little bit. Do that now for each topic.

Now, reread both columns. The first column is labeled, "Things I've Been Taught" (old beliefs, brain chatter), and the second column, "What I Really Believe," when I don't listen to the chatter or old tapes in my head. As you read through these again after you've completed the exercise, you may find that you have quite a few different beliefs from those you have been taught. There's nothing wrong with that. Acknowledge the fact that you have your own ideas about things and that it is okay. You may be getting an *awareness* that you have been denying the 'real' you, and that you've been living your life based on someone else's belief system long enough. This exercise is your opportunity to find out exactly what you believe. This is an opportunity for you to stand on your own two feet and live your life your way.

I will give you fair warning. Inner work or self-discovery will not be the easiest thing you've ever done. First of all, many people simply won't understand what it is you're doing especially those who have given you that old belief system. They will feel betrayed and it will probably put a strain on some of your relationships. You may experience doubt, loneliness and some dark nights of the soul. But if you want freedom in your life, do this work.

Since you're making such great progress, let's not stop here. On another page in your notebook, begin to answer some of these following questions or any questions that you come up with on your own. This may take hours, days, or years. It doesn't matter. I promise that by doing this exercise and by taking the time to answer these questions honestly, you can change your life.

Self-Esteem and Personal Power

Am I in the job I really want to be in or is there something else I would be completely passionate about doing?

What's keeping me from leaving this job and doing what I truly want to do?

Am I afraid to fail?

Am I afraid to succeed?

Am I afraid of what others will say or think?

Relationships

What have I been told to believe about sex?

What do I believe about healthy communication?

Prosperity

What have I been told about money?

What have I been told about how it's best to make money?

What do I believe about making money?

What do I believe about saving money?

What do I believe about spending money?

Health and Body

What do I believe about myself?

What have I been told about working out?

Do I believe it's selfish to spend time on myself?

What have I been told about taking time to meditate and relax?

Grief and Loss

What have I been told about showing my emotions?

What do I believe happens when someone dies?

Am I afraid of death?

Do I believe in an afterlife?

Spirituality

Who or what is God to me?

Where does my definition of God live?

What does God look like?

Is God male or female, neither, or both?

Does my God judge, think, punish?

Am I beginning to doubt what I've been taught my whole life?

Is that okay?

Do I live my life based on what other people will think, especially my
family and my church?

Example: Forgiveness. I was always taught that we had to ask God
for forgiveness. I was also taught that based on our behavior, he may
or may not forgive and that we wouldn't know for sure until we were
judged at the final judgment. It was only then that we would know if
we were forgiven and would make it to heaven or that we were not forgiven and go to hell. Well, that belief wasn't working for me because I
was miserable and felt guilty and scared all the time. I needed to change
that belief into something that made my life better. So I did.

My new belief is that The Universe/God/Energy does not have a
conscious mind and the ability to think. Therefore this Energy is inca-
pable of judging or forgiving, and so it is I who judges me and it is I who
forgives me. Forgiveness only comes when I forgive myself. Forgiveness
has nothing to do with a God up in the sky. It comes from within.
Otherwise, how could atheists forgive? Once I formed this new belief, I
slept better, had fewer body aches and pains, and enjoyed much clearer
thinking. I found some wonderful self-forgiving exercises to do and began to do them religiously.

Example: I was also taught from an early age that if I didn't follow
the teachings of the Adventist church, the devil would have a heyday
with me. I was also taught that if I did follow the teachings of the
church that I would be a threat to the devil and he would certainly
try to destroy me. For goodness sakes! Either way, the devil was after
me and I was in trouble. But when I began to question that old belief system and after I started forming my own beliefs about who and
what the devil actually was, I completely changed that old belief into

something life-empowering for me. When I began to understand that God and the devil were simply opposites in the form of Energy, I realized that there were no human thoughts involved. I realized my own mind was in control of both ends of this spectrum of Energy. I was the one who formed positive thoughts or negative thoughts. I controlled both the high frequencies of Energy moving and the low frequencies of Energy moving. God changed from being a judging angry old man up in the sky to a positive flowing Energy in my life. The devil changed from a twisted evil monger lurking around seeking those he may devour into negative Energy or thoughts. When this downloaded into my brain, I experienced a burst of personal power and personal freedom like never before! It was awesome.

But I didn't stop there. I continued to fine-tune my beliefs on this subject. My personal belief is that it isn't the old religious devil that is tormenting people. Rather, it's the negative thoughts of our own minds. It isn't the judgmental religious God who is helping or causing us to succeed. It's our own positive thoughts, discipline and will-power. I believe it's time we all begin to take credit for what we accomplish and to also take responsibility for our failures. When we do, we are taking personal responsibility to a new level, and we will experience the reality and the true meaning of taking responsibility for our own life. That's when we will experience personal power.

Since I had formed new beliefs about Universal Energy and was learning how to work with it, I began to form even more new beliefs. I now believed in the Universal Law of manifestation or the power of intention, also known as the "Power of Attraction." When I know what I want, in detail, I ask for it, visualize it and feel it happening using all five senses. Then I allow it to happen, and I am grateful for getting it, even if it hasn't happened yet. I know I'll get it. This is the same teaching of Jesus, Yogis, many Christians, Abraham, and many others. I started believing that **everything** is moving, vibrating Energy and that different forms of Energy vibrate at different speeds. That means that words are Energy, and I began to *realize* how extremely important words are, as well as how we use them. I now understood what Jesus meant when he said to plant seeds because words are seeds, and seeds are Energy that will grow and will manifest whatever it is you planted, negative or positive.

As my interest continued to grow in the study of Energy and how it works, I began to wonder if Jesus and all the miracles he performed were results of his mastery in the use of Energy. Yes, that is exactly what I believed. I believe that he had a deep understanding of Universal or God Energy and knew exactly how to work with it. I believe he was a master at it, and I believe he was a master teacher of it while he was on this earth. There have been many other great teachers through the ages and I know now that they had the same knowledge as Jesus concerning Energy, maybe even more. These other teachers are not considered to be Christian, though, and are therefore not mentioned in the Bible. That doesn't mean they didn't exist. They certainly did and they did amazing work. Many of these teachers are American Indians; some are Buddhists, some Hindus and there are many others. One in particular I love to read about is Paramahansa Yogananda. Like Jesus, he was a master teacher who performed miracles and had many followers. In fact, it was while reading some of his teachings and books that I began to truly understand who Jesus was and why he did what he did during his life. I began to think about the fact that if everything vibrates, then our emotions must have vibrations as well. As I continued to read and study everything I could get my hands on, I felt very settled in my new belief. This is why I don't believe that God is a thinking entity. God, as some people call it, is an energetic vibrating force that scientifically, and without fail, reacts only to the energetic vibrations that we send out. If you send out yuck, you get yuck back. If you vibrate love and peace, you get love and peace back. If you send out financial gifts, you get financial gifts back. If you send out gossiping words, you get them back. It's very basic and very simple. If you vibrate need, you will live in need. If you vibrate prosperity, you will live in prosperity. I like to tell people: "Think thin, be thin; think fat, be fat; think depressed, be depressed; think happy, be happy." Whatever you think, that you are and that you will be. Since our thoughts and emotions are Energy and have specific Energy patterns according to Universal Laws, they absolutely affect us physically. That's why I firmly believe that the first step to healing physically is to begin healing emotionally.

Think about that for a second: The first step to healing physically is to begin to heal emotionally. That means you have a lot of power and control over the ability of your body to heal itself. Wow! You have the power to heal yourself. Did you know that? But you don't just have power over your own health. You have power, through your emotions and thoughts, to control your finances, your relationships, and your career.

You can begin to see now why it's so important to know what you don't want, to know what it is you do want, and to make a conscious decision to dwell on what it is you want. What you dwell on is what you're going to get... every time . . . it's Universal Law. You don't get it because you believe in God or go to church on Saturday or Sunday or because your volunteer for special groups. You get what you think because that's what you're vibrating. You have more control than you ever realized. That also means that you have more responsibility than you ever thought you had. Be aware that with more power comes more responsibility.

Your thoughts, in fact, have so much energetic power that when you walk into a room and project your thoughts, those thoughts influence everyone else in the room and even your reality. So that means, in fact, that you, not anyone else, are in control of your own reality.

So among the many questions I asked myself, I wondered what I thought self-*realization* was, and I actually had an answer of my own.

God/Energy/Spirit/Universe/*qi* (pronounced "chi" by the Chinese) or whatever name works for you, is not outside of me. It is not separate from me. That means that if I believe that God/Energy/Spirit/Universe is in me, then, I am in it, and that means we are one. That means I am Energy. I am Spirit. I am Universe. I would say I am God, but I still have a few religious tapes that go off in my head when I use that phrase. So I just don't say it. Anyway, my point is: I am capable of anything once I align correctly with Energy/God/Spirit. You are capable of anything once you align correctly with Energy/God/Spirit. I can only explain this so far, though, because the definition of God or Energy or Universe or Spirit or Force or Higher Power cannot be put into words. It can only be "*realized*." And it is "*realized*" by each individual however they "*realize*" it. What that source or power means to me may not be what it means to you. And that's okay! That's why it's called "self" *realization*. You have to *realize* it, the source, or God, for your "self."

Make sure you have taken the time to write down your beliefs in the previous exercise. If you did, let's move on. First, you wrote your old beliefs (mind chatter) in column one. Then, in column two, you wrote what **you** really believe, or what you would like to believe even though you may not be living with that belief now. I'd like for you to continue with these two columns. Draw a line across your page, and under both columns, write what you would **like** to believe about each subject you've written about. Write what you'd like to believe if you had absolute power and freedom. These beliefs may be the same as what are in column two or they may be completely different. Write what you would believe if no one would judge you, or be angry with you. Write whatever you want and write without any fear. Write with courage. Some of your thoughts may not change. That's okay. Remember, your beliefs need to be what you *feel* is true for you, not what you *think* is true or what you've been *told* is true. What *feels* true for you? Write it down. You can change it any time because, after all, it's your truth. Now go to work. If you haven't completed this work, please don't read any further until you do.

Exercise 1.4

Write what you would like to believe.

The next step, which may be a little harder, is to start living with those new beliefs that you've just written down. I'll share a few helpful hints. Begin, by writing down, in short phrases, all your new beliefs.

Exercise 1.5

Write all your new beliefs in short phrases.

For example: "I now believe that it's fun to make money," or "I now believe that the Universe will always provide me with what I need and want," or

"I deserve a passionate and exciting relationship."

Start writing your new beliefs now. When you've finished, consider typing or writing them on pieces of paper and placing them around your home or office.

Exercise 1.6

Type or write your new phrases on cards or paper and place them around your house or work.

Once you've written or typed your new empowering beliefs, it's time to begin speaking them out loud and to begin training your subconscious mind to believe everything you've written. It's time to get your powerful Energy flowing in the right direction!

Here's your homework check list:

1. Be aware of your words throughout the day and write then down.
2. Write some of your core beliefs you've been taught in column one.
3. Write your true beliefs in column two.
4. Write what you would like to believe.
5. Write all your new beliefs in short phrases.
6. Type or write your new phrases on cards or paper and place them around your house or work.

I hope you took the time to do each of the previous exercises. If you really want to change and heal your life, then the time has come to begin asking yourself the tough questions. It's time for self-discovery and self-*realization*. It's time to live an authentic life. It's time to ask the questions you were probably told never to ask, or thought you would never ask, or were afraid to ask. But here is one of the biggest keys to living a fulfilled life: You have to be brutally honest with yourself when you ask and when you answer these questions or you're wasting your time. Better yet, you're wasting your life. You cannot just skim over questions like these and write out what you've always been told or what you think you "might" believe, or what you've even read in this book or other books. If you truly want to empower yourself and liberate your life you must take the time to hold these questions in your mind. Ponder them and answer them for yourself. It may take hours, days, or years for you to answer one question but it will be worth it.

When you complete this work, you're ready for the next chapter.

CHAPTER 2

THE POWER OF YOUR WORDS

Sticks and stones may break your bones
but words hurt even worse.
~ Vicky~

Affirmations are your thoughts or beliefs put into words. They are spoken statements, living and vibrating with Energy. Another way to look at affirmations is that they are words with emotion in them. Emotions also vibrate with Energy. Whether you *realize* it or not, you affirm things, all day, every day. Unfortunately, the majority of people affirm negative things without much *awareness*, for instance, "I hate my job," "I'm so fat," "I never can get a lucky break," "I just can't get ahead," or, "I'll never get out of debt." If a person continues to say that he will never get out of debt, he never will get out of debt. It's what he believes. It's what he is affirming, and he is affirming those words with emotion. Emotion makes words very powerful, and what you send out, you will attract back.

STOP in your tracks right now! To gain control over your life, you must be *aware* of the words you speak. Please put a watch over your words from this moment forward. Humor me and say this right now. Say it out loud even if you have to whisper it. Let your ears hear it. *I put a watch over my words and say only what contributes to my highest good. I am aware of everything that comes out of my mouth.*

Did you say it? If you didn't, say it now. There is no getting around the fact that what comes out of your mouth comes to pass. I'll say that again. What comes out of your mouth comes to pass. This isn't just something I've made up. This is one of our Universal Laws. It doesn't matter who you are, how much money you have, how smart you are, what religion you belong to, or what color skin you have. You will get what you say. Guaranteed!

So, don't you think it's critically important that you pay close attention to what is coming out of your mouth every day? I thought you would agree. So, let's get right to it.

Begin each day *realizing* how powerful your words are. Then begin to listen to what you're saying and what other people are saying. Each day, when you get up, set your intention to not let your words be tossed about aimlessly. They carry far too much power to throw them around without any thought behind them. Choose your words wisely. They are extremely powerful. They are living, vibrating particles of Energy.

The Psalmist of the Bible in Psalms 141:3 said "Set a guard, O Lord, over my mouth; Keep watch over the door of my lips." Did you ever wonder why he said that? I think he wrote that because he must have known how much power words have in them.

Proverbs 21:23 says, "He who guards his mouth and his tongue, guards his soul from troubles." This is another example of the power of words.

Because I was raised reading the Bible and because I spent twelve years in private religious school, a lot of the "old tapes" that I hear in my head come directly from the Bible. Even though I don't believe the Bible to be completely accurate because it has been translated so many times, I still believe there is some good advice in it.

I find it interesting that throughout the Bible there are many verses and parables concerning the power of words or affirmations and about the Law of Attraction. For instance, Matthew 7:7–12 says "Ask and it shall be given to you, seek and you shall find, knock and it shall be opened to you. For every one who asks receives, and he who seeks finds, and to him who knocks, it shall be opened." To me, that means if we ask for, act on, and believe for what we want, it will come to us. It's a Universal Law, and it works 100% of the time for every single person regardless of race, religion, or income.

"And Jesus said to the centurion, 'go your way; let it be done to you as you have believed.' And the servant was healed that very hour." Matthew 8:13. Jesus was telling this man that the Universal Law known as the power of intention was at work within him. To the extent that you believe you will receive. Again, this is guaranteed regardless of who you are.

Matthew 21:21–22. "Truly I say to you, if you have faith, and do not doubt, you shall not only do what was done to the fig tree, but even if you say to this mountain, 'Be taken up and cast into the sea', it shall happen. And everything you ask in prayer, believing, you shall receive." Again, Universal Law being taught by Jesus.

I like this one too: Matthew 12:33–37 says that the words that come out of your mouth reveal your character. "Either make the tree good, and its fruit good; or make the tree rotten, and its fruit rotten; for the tree is known by its fruit. You brood of vipers, how can you, being evil, speak what is good? For the mouth speaks out of that which fills the heart. The good man out of his good treasure brings forth what is good; and the evil man out of his evil treasure brings forth what is evil. And I say to you, that every careless word that men shall speak they shall render account for in the 'day of judgment'. For by your words you shall be justified, and by your words you shall be condemned." Our words are powerful!

Since everyone is entitled to interpret things the way they want, I interpret this to say that you either make your life good because you make good decisions and by speaking positive words, or you make your life rotten because of rotten decisions and by speaking negative words. Your life experience is based on the kind of decisions you make and the words you speak. Whatever is in your heart or on your mind the most is what will come out your mouth in the form of words. People who experience good things in life speak good, uplifting, empowering, and positive words because that's what they believe. People who experience bad things in life speak negative, hateful, disempowering words because that's what they believe. We are each individually responsible and accountable for our own words and therefore for the outcome of our own lives. The 'day of judgment' is today and every day. The 'day of judgment' is not a specific time within a twenty-four hour period when a god out there somewhere will judge us. You are the judge of your own life each and every day.

Today, take inventory of what you're saying. I'll bet that your life reflects your words. Try to become *aware* of the times when you say something negative. It will draw exactly what you don't want into your life. Change it to what you do want and say it out loud immediately. For example, let's say you're at the gym working out and you see someone walk through the locker room and they are absolutely the definition of health and fitness. You turn to your friend and say, "I'll never look like that. I don't have the time or the discipline it takes." You're right! If you continue to say those words, you never will look like that. Instead, say "I'm going to do whatever it takes to look like her. I know I can do it."

You must understand that your brain hears and believes everything that comes out of your mouth. If you said you'll never look that good, your brain now believes that you'll never look like that other person and it will go about creating situations to make your words come true. You probably will be too tired to work out in the morning, or too busy to work out in the evening. You'll more than likely crave all the foods that are bad for you, and when you do eat a balanced meal, you'll eat way too much. Then what happens? You say, "See, I told you I would never look like that," over and over. There you have it. You got exactly what you said. The person who looks so good, by the way, has probably figured out how to say, "I feel so much better when I work out. It actually energizes me," "I eat only foods that are good for me." "I never crave sweets." Guess what? Their brain heard their words and created situations to make them come true. Like Energy attracts like Energy.

It's a very simple Universal Law. All you have to do is be *aware* of what you're saying and be in charge of your words. Universal Energy will do the rest. What you send out, you get back. Don't complicate it. Now, let's make some positive changes in your life and let's begin with your mouth.

Take as much time as you need, whether its thirty minutes, or three days to do this exercise. In your notebook, write down what you really want in your life. Write down everything you can think of. What kind of family do you want? What type of work do you want to be doing? How much money do you want to make a year? What do you want your body to look like? Be very clear about what you want. After you answer each question, go back and write out an affirmation or phrase that says you already have it or are experiencing it. The affirmation needs to be written as if it's already happening. I'll give you some examples and then you take it from there. If you say, "I hope to have" or "I wish," then, you'll continue to bring only a wish or a hope. It will continue to be just out of your reach.

Exercise 2.1

Write down what you really want in life.

Exercise 2.2

Write an affirmation that states you already have each of your desire.

Example: What does your dream relationship look like?

Write the affirmation that says you already have your dream relationship. Something like: *I have and am so grateful for my loving relationship*

31

with _____. *I have the most wonderful husband (boyfriend, girl-friend, etc.) I could ever hope for. We respect one another, trust one another, understand and love one another and our communication is simply the best.*

Or write your own.

What do you want your family life to be like?

What do you need to affirm that says you already have it.? Write it down.

What type of work do you want to be doing?

Write your affirmation that reflects you having your dream job.

How much money do you want to make a year?

Affirmation: *I am so grateful that I easily make* _____ *dollars a year.*

At first it feels like you're lying to yourself, but if you continue to say these words, you will soon start believing it. The Universal Energy will attract it into your life, and you'll be on your way to making just what you have affirmed. Don't give up and don't quit too soon.

How do you want your body to look?

Write it out: I appreciate my strong, fit body.

Now be realistic here. If you're 5'6" and want to be 5'9", I'm afraid that's universally impossible. Sorry. What you could do, though, is wear three inch heels and affirm, "*When I wear my three inch heels, I am 5'9"*. Seriously, though, write down, within reason, what you want to look like, and then affirm something like:

I easily maintain my ideal size and weight. I eat only appropriate portions of foods that support me and keep me strong and healthy. I enjoy working out regularly. I am disciplined. I am full of Energy and I am fit.

What type of friends do you want?
Write it down.

Where do you want to be spiritually?

Example: *I am open to many truths, and I search and study for my own beliefs in my own way. I am becoming more aware on a daily basis that life is good and everything is as it should be.* Or whatever suits you better.

Anything else? Write it down.

Take the time today to answer as many of these questions as you can. If you don't finish it today, work on it each day until you have a list of new empowering affirmations.

Do something else for me right now. Say out loud or whisper if you don't want anyone to hear you, "*I regularly affirm the life of my dreams.* Good!

Next assignment. Whether it's now or later, write or type all of your above affirmations on index cards or pieces of paper and place them where you will see them throughout your day. The bathroom mirror is one of my favorites along with the refrigerator. I have even put one on the door going from the garage into my house. Make more than one set and place them in your office, car, or wherever you spend a lot of time. When you see them, speak them out loud.

Exercise 2.3

Write all your new affirmation on cards or pieces of paper and place them where you will see them throughout the day.

You are *realizing* and becoming *aware* that your words and thoughts create your reality. You are learning that you alone are in complete control of your words and your thoughts and therefore you alone are in charge of your own reality.

Remember that what you send out in words, thoughts, and emotions will come back to you. It's guaranteed! It's Universal Law.

I'm wondering as you do this work, if you might be having thoughts like, "But I really don't believe that I'll ever look good," or "I'll never get that job I've been wanting." Did the little voice in your head say something like that when you were doing the above exercise? What it is telling you is that you MUST change that particular belief. If you believe you can't lose weight, then you've got to change that belief or you will never lose weight. Let's affirm a new belief about that right now. Instead of believing that, *"I'll never look good,"* change your new belief to be, *"I easily maintain my ideal size and weight. I love and care for my body."* If you send those words out, it will begin working for you immediately. Now, stick with it. As your belief changes, so will your words, and so will your body.

Remember, earlier in the book, when you did some work on your beliefs about money? If you had disempowering beliefs about money and you wrote a new belief, this next step is how you will remove the old belief and install your new one. You do it with your words. You will need to stop using your old phrases and negative affirmations that you've been using all your life and begin using your new phrases and your new affirmations. This is how you change beliefs and how you start turning your life around.

Let's take each disempowering belief you wrote down earlier and change it into something positive.

Money

Example of old belief:

Money is the root of all evil. Money doesn't grow on trees. Only the
  rich get richer.
Example of new belief:
Money flows easily into my life.
It's a joy to make money.
Money allows me to give and help others.
My work fulfills me completely.
Write more of your own.

Do this in all areas of your life - physically, emotionally, socially,
and spiritually. The previous exercises in the book set the stage for your
new beliefs and affirmations. Now it's time to make it all happen. Take
the time now to write or type your new affirmations that you will be
posting around your house.

Have fun making these changes. Make it a daily habit. Make it a
lifestyle.

Additional affirmations:

Accomplishing

I was not born to be defeated. I was born to accomplish.
I accomplish whatever I set out to do with ease.
Today I begin a new life.
With every breath, I release all that binds me and keeps me from ac-
  complishing my purpose for this life.
I have the power and strength to handle everything in my life.

I have enough time and Energy to do everything I need and choose to do.

I trust myself.

I now take daily steps in the direction of my goals.

I easily accept my dreams and goals with wisdom and grace.

I accept change with ease.

I now embrace good habits. Good habits are the key to success.

I now choose to rise above any obstacles that stand in my way.

I speak positive words daily and they seep into my conscious mind, and more importantly, into my unconscious mind where they have taken root and drive me in the direction of my dreams and purpose.

I am always in the right place at the right time.

Loving and Being Loved

I have love in my heart.

I have forgiveness in my heart.

I send love and forgiveness to those who have done me wrong.

I love, approve of and accept myself.

I am loving and lovable.

I love the poor and I love the rich.

I love the plain and I love the beautiful.

I love the young and I love the old.

I have an endless supply of love to give.

I attract positive loving people into my life.

A Grateful Heart

Today I am grateful for...

List all the things you are grateful for.

Success and Financial Freedom

I deserve the best of everything and I accept it now.
I am constantly making positive changes in my life.
I deserve to have my ideal lifestyle and I accept it now.
I am open to the endless flow of prosperity.
All my needs are met.
I now have abundance thinking.
Abundance is everywhere.
I now release old belief patterns regarding money, need, and limitations.

Relationships

I deserve my ideal relationship.
I am desirable.
I am sexy.
I am loveable.
I make friends easily.
I am a good friend to others.
I easily manifest all that is needed for me to have my ideal relationship and my ideal lifestyle.
I have a positive influence on everyone I meet.
I experience love wherever I go.

Miscellaneous

I release old beliefs and patterns and am moving forward with my life.
I deserve all that is good in my life.
I look at all situations through eyes of love and see all situations as learning experiences.

The Universe always provides for me, and I constantly allow an abundance of love, health, wealth, happiness, and peace to flow through me.

I am free from guilt, fear, and punishment and those things no longer affect me.

I am healthy and strong physically, emotionally, financially, and spiritually.

I deserve the best of everything, and I accept it now.

I deserve pleasures, happiness and contentment and I accept them now.

My life is full of abundance, health, and happiness.

Whatever I need to know is being revealed to me.

I think only positive thoughts and speak only positive words, knowing that my thoughts and words create my life.

I am willing to release any and all old disempowering beliefs that no longer serve me.

I am open to new beliefs that empower my life.

I always make wise decisions.

I appreciate.

I love.

I am at peace.

I am a forgiving person.

I am powerful

I am excited.

I am willing.

I accept myself.

I love myself.

I am empowered.

I am liberated.

I am free.

Chapter Exercises

1. Write down what you really want in life.
2. Write an affirmation that states you already have each of your desires.
3. Write all your new affirmations on cards or pieces of paper and place them where you will see them throughout the day

CHAPTER 3

AFFIRMATIONS

I believe in myself and in the
Universe (God).
~Vicky~

H ere are some helpful affirmations to help you reprogram your thoughts and confirm your new beliefs.

Spirituality

I look at all situations through eyes of love, and all situations are learning experiences.

I enjoy who I am.

The Universe (or God) always provides for me, and I constantly allow an abundance of love, health, wealth, happiness, and peace to flow through me.

I am free from guilt, fear, and punishment, and it no longer affects me.

I am a forgiving person.

I am free.

I believe in myself and in the Universe (God).

Whatever I need to know will be revealed to me.

I am responsible for my reality.

I am free to change my beliefs.

Self-Esteem and Personal Power

I deeply appreciate and accept myself.

I am excited.

I accept myself.

I have an excellent memory.

My creativity is unlimited.

I am focused.

I am successful.

I can do anything I put my mind to.

I am releasing old beliefs and patterns and am moving forward with my life

I love myself unconditionally.

I am releasing old beliefs and patterns and am moving forward with my life.

I deserve pleasures, happiness and contentment, and I accept it now.

I always make wise decisions.

I am powerful.

I deserve the very best life has to offer.

I am confident and self-assured.

I am proud of my results and comfortable with my successes and my failures.

I am a good person.

I do my best, and my best is good enough.

I trust the decisions I make.

I trust the Divine guidance I am receiving.

I acknowledge my ability and responsibility to make a positive difference in the world.

I actively embrace the opportunities that come with change.

I am true to my personal vision.

I am willing to take the risks necessary to live my life openly and honestly.

I give myself permission to do what I love.

I am constantly making positive changes in my life.

I was not born to be defeated. I was born to accomplish.

I accomplish whatever I set out to do with ease.

Today I begin a new life.

With every breath I release all that binds me and keeps me from accomplishing my purpose for this life.

I have the power and strength to handle everything in my life.

I trust myself.

I take daily steps in the direction of my goals.

I easily accept my dreams and goals with wisdom and grace.

I accept change with ease.

I now embrace good habits which are the key to my success.

I now choose to rise above any obstacles that come my way.

I will repeat these words daily so they will seep into my conscious mind and more importantly into my un-conscious mind where they will take root and drive me in the direction of my dreams and purpose.

Relationships

I deserve my ideal relationship.

I am desirable.

I am sexy.

I enjoy romance and deep intimacy with a loving partner.

I make friends easily.

I have honest and healthy friendships.

I am a good friend to others.

I easily manifest all that is needed for me to have my ideal relationship and my ideal lifestyle.

I experience love wherever I go.

It's easy for me to give love to others.

It's easy for me to receive love from others.

I am worthy of an intimate, passionate relationship.

I am ready for a powerful, intimate relationship in my life now.

It's okay for me to express my truth in a relationship.

It's okay for me to grow and change in a relationship.

I have love in my heart.

I send love to those who have done me wrong.

I love, approve and accept myself.

I am loving and lovable.

I love the poor I love the rich.

I love the plain and I love the beautiful.

I love the young and I love the old.

I have an endless supply of love to give.

I attract positive loving people into my life.

Prosperity

I deserve the best of everything, and I accept it now.

I deserve all that is good in my life.

My life is full of abundance, health, and happiness.

I deserve to have my ideal lifestyle, and I accept it now.

I am open to the endless flow of prosperity.

I deserve to have all the money I need.

All my needs are met.

I have abundance thinking.

Abundance is everywhere.

I now release old belief patterns of money, lack, and limitations.

I trust myself to manage money honestly and sensibly.

It is okay for me to enjoy money.

I enjoy making lots of money and spending it.

I can make all the money I need doing a job that I love.

It is okay to have more money than I need.

Money flows easily into my life.

It's a joy to make money.

Money allows me to give and help others.

My work fulfills me completely.

Health and Body

I accept my age, and I age with grace, beauty, and vitality.

My body heals itself naturally and quickly.

I am healthy and strong physically, emotionally, financially, and spiritually.

I accept health as being a natural part of my life.

I am a good person and deserve to have a healthy body.

I love and accept my body as it is and as it changes.

I am full of energy, tireless, and move through life with ease.

I easily maintain my ideal weight and size.

I eat only the amounts my body needs.

I eat healthy nutritional foods.

I feel safe, secure, and confident when my body is slim and trim.

I sleep peacefully and arise each morning refreshed and energized.

Grief and Loss

I release all guilt, shame and blame resulting from my past thoughts and actions.

I forgive myself.

I fill my mind with positive, nurturing and healing thoughts.

I acknowledge my feelings as a necessary part of my healing process.

I know when it is time to let go, and I do.

Everything happens in Divine Order.

I have faith in myself and my future.

A Grateful Heart

I am grateful for so much.

I am at peace.

Today I am grateful for . . . .

CHAPTER 4

BELIEVE, THINK, SPEAK, EXPECT

You are what you believe you are.
You do what you think you can do.
You get what you say.
~Vicky~

Now that you've written out your beliefs; you've no doubt shocked yourself slightly. Do your everyday life, job situation, family and other relationships, finances and your health represent your old beliefs and the words you have been speaking? I guarantee they do. You now understand that we create with our beliefs, our thoughts, and our words, the situations and reality that we live. If you change your beliefs, thoughts, and words, you will change your life. You create your experiences for tomorrow, next week, next month, next year, and for the rest of your life. You are in charge.

If you believe that you aren't good enough, you'll never be good enough. If you believe you don't deserve, you won't receive. Instead, begin to believe that you are worthy to have what you want by saying, "I am worthy and I deserve all I desire." Begin telling yourself that "I am willing to let go of old disempowering beliefs about myself." Say, "I approve and accept myself. I am capable of doing all that I desire and more." Tell yourself this until you really believe it. Your life and your reality will follow your words and your thoughts. Do this and watch for miracles to happen in your life.

You are in the midst of such powerful change that nothing will be able to hold you back. Good for you! There will be times when you slip backwards and use negative and self-defeating words; everyone does at times. What's important is that you immediately catch yourself and take control over your mouth. Stop and make yourself think happy thoughts instead of sad thoughts. Make yourself think about how great it feels when you are healthy and slim instead of how it feels to be tired and overweight. Think what you want!

Begin this very moment to make changes in your beliefs, thoughts, and words. Do your very best. If you fail on a particular day, be gentle with yourself and pick up where you left off.

Remember:

If you want a healthy life, think and speak healthy thoughts.
If you want prosperity, think and speak prosperous thoughts.
If you want a loving relationship, think and speak loving thoughts.
Whatever you want, think and speak those thoughts.

AND

If you don't want lack, do not think and speak of lack.
If you don't want criticism, don't speak words or think thoughts of criticism toward yourself or others.

To have the awareness and catch yourself thinking and speaking disempowering emotions is one thing but taking action to stop it and change it is another. From firsthand experience, I realize that this can be very difficult to do.

When I was in my thirties, I was diagnosed with a medically incurable condition that the doctors said would have me in a wheelchair by the time I was forty. I was prescribed an array of prescription drugs and told that they would ease my symptoms but would not address what was causing those symptoms. What I learned about those drugs is that their side effects were as bad as, if not worse than, the current symptoms that I was experiencing. What I really needed to do was find out what was "causing" my symptoms and go to work on that.

That's exactly what I did. The first place I started my healing was by getting control of my thoughts. My thoughts were those of fear; fear of what I thought was going to happen because I was a fitness instructor and trainer, and owned and operated a large fitness facility, spa and salon. I was also very active in other recreation sports. This diagnosis was almost more than I could handle. Fortunately, I realized that I needed to control my thoughts and my words about what was going on in my body so that I wouldn't actually "make" it happen. It was one of the most difficult things I have ever done. I made a decision to not speak of the diagnosis or the outcome as if it would happen or was happening. Instead, I chose to speak and think only thoughts of healing and health. How did I do that? I'm glad you asked.

If you've never consciously taken control of your thoughts before, it is difficult to begin but it is not impossible. What I had to do was find a way to take my mind off the negative situation I was facing. At first I tried to avoid those thoughts by working harder and more hours. That didn't work because I wasn't physically capable of doing so. This is when I found out how amazing meditation is. I started out by reading several books on meditation. I then tried my very best to sit and quiet my mind. I couldn't do it. I tried everything from lying on the floor with nature sounds playing in my ears to sitting in lotus position to staring into the flame of a candle. I even tried staring into the flame of a candle. No matter what I did, I could not quiet my mind and control my thoughts of fear. Finally, I was introduced to guided meditation. It worked like a miracle. By listening to guided meditations I was able to distract my mind for an hour at a time. I was hooked. Each time I would end my session, my body felt lighter and more alive. I had some amazing experiences during those first couple of years learning to meditate. My point is this; you must find a healthy way to distract your mind from thinking negative thoughts and fill it with positive ones instead. You must then make certain you speak positive words instead of negative words. What do you think would have happened if I would have walked around everyday telling people what was supposed to happen to me? What if I would have said, "I'm probably going to be in a wheelchair by the time I'm forty?" I would have been in a wheelchair by the time I was forty. Why? Because that what I would have believed.

I am so grateful that I learned the Law of Attraction before something that devastating happened. Our beliefs, thoughts, and words carry more powerful energy than most people realize.

Gaining control of my thoughts and words was only the first step in my healing. I had to go on then to find out what was "causing" that horrible disease. What I found out was that I was operating under a very old and very disempowering belief system that was so unhealthy that it was making me physically sick. My job, if I wanted to stay on my feet and live a long and healthy life, was to change that belief system. I did. I am healthy and will continue to be. That's what I believe, what I think, and what I speak. I write about my healing journey more in depth in my book *Changing the Face of God*.

Know that you too have unlimited Power over your life my friend. If you are willing to do what it takes to know what you believe, have the courage to change any beliefs that disempower you, and discipline yourself so you can control your mind and your mouth, you too can change and heal your life, physically, emotionally, and spiritually. I trust you will.

ABOUT THE AUTHOR

For nearly thirty years, Vicky Thurlow has inspired tens of thousands of individuals with her passion for life. As a certified fitness instructor, personal trainer, model, author, entrepreneur and business owner, she fully understands the importance of discipline, fitness, and beauty from the inside out.

Overcoming her cult-like religious upbringing and battling a medically incurable condition, Vicky's unrelenting desire to heal herself and help others enabled her to successfully learn to trust holistic healing techniques, and change her life forever. She energetically lives her purpose and openly shares her experiences to help others connect to an array of healing techniques and resources.

For more information about Vicky's work, books, guided meditations, CDs, DVDs, workshops, and healing resources, please visit her Web site: http://www.pursuitofhealing.com.

TO PURCHASE ADDITIONAL COPIES OF THIS BOOK

Contact DVT Investments
2800 Printers Way,
Grand Junction, Colorado 81506

or visit http://www.pursuitofhealing.com

NOTES

NOTES

NOTES